THE MAN ON THE TOWER

Arkansas Poetry Award Series

THE MAN
ON THE TOWER

Poems by Charles Rafferty

THE UNIVERSITY OF ARKANSAS PRESS

FAYETTEVILLE   1995

Designed by Gail Carter

☉ The paper used in this publication meets the minimum
requirements of the American National Standard for
Permanence of Paper for Printed Library Materials
Z39.48-1984.

Library of Congress Cataloging-in-Publication Data
Rafferty, Charles, 1965–
    The man on the tower : poems / by Charles Rafferty.
      p. cm. — (Arkansas poetry award series)
    ISBN 1-55728-339-7. — ISBN 1-55728-340-0 (pbk.)
    I. Title. II. Series.
PS3568.A378M36 1992
811'.54—dc20   94-37208
                          CIP

For Wendy

ACKNOWLEDGMENTS

Grateful acknowledgment is made to the editors of the following journals in which these poems first appeared: *Lactuca:* "The Prediction," "The Man in the Car Explains His Obsession"; *Yarrow:* "On Being Told Again That My Position Could Be No Further from the Truth"; *Without Halos:* "The Dishwasher," "The Silent Man Speaks"; *Parting Gifts:* "Finding Her"; *Trestle Creek Review:* "The Proposal"; *Duckabush Journal:* "Story of the Escape Artist"; *The Paper Bag:* "Story of the Man Waking Up"; *Rag Mag:* "The Mammoth"; *A.K.A. Magazine:* "Story of the Man on the Tracks"; *Piedmont Literary Journal:* "The Corner of Past Loves"; *Alchemy:* "The Arsonist Tells His Story to the Attorney"; *Stockpot:* "The Proposal," "Devotion," "Finding Her"; *Riverrun:* "To Men in Pursuit of Uninterested Women"; *Thirteen Poetry Magazine:* "The Box"; *Epiphany: The Ogalala Review:* "The Arsonist Tells His Story to the Attorney"; *The Cape Rock:* "The Man Who Invented Urinal Mints Attends His Class Reunion"; *Poetry East:* "Story of the Man Whose Tastes Were Too Refined"; and *Painted Bride Quarterly:* "The Man Whose Luck Is Changing," "The Man without Passion Arrives at the Grand Canyon."

CONTENTS

I. THE CRACKLING OF CASTANETS

II. AN EXPLOSION OF GREEN SURRENDER

III. SEVERAL SONG-FILLED MINUTES

I. THE CRACKLING OF CASTANETS

THE ARSONIST TELLS HIS STORY
TO THE ATTORNEY

It got so bad I never saw
the same girl twice.
When I told one about the barn
I burned—how the flames
slid across the rafters,
exciting the whole frame
into a frenzy it hadn't felt
since it was trees on a stormy night—
she made me stop the car.
And her unkissed thighs
walked back to town, leaving me
my hands, a hot silence
that had to touch everything.
I eventually stopped dating.
I spent my Saturday afternoons
scouting out buildings
that reminded me of girls—ugly girls
who had asked their mothers
for makeup and been refused.
That's where I came in,
like some big-hearted Avon lady,
moistening the floorboards
with gasoline, touching a match
to some place appropriate.
I did it for the beauty
and for the fire that came,

transforming a shack
to a red-haired woman
in an orange dress—
who kicked her hem above her head
to the crackling of castanets.

THE MAN WHO WOULD BE ANONYMOUS

I have filed my fingerprints down
till they are smooth
as ten pink pearls.
I have burned my wallet,
peeled the women from my biceps,
and plucked out all
my prominent moles. Now,
without luggage or license plates,
I have pointed my car
at a world that I can claim.
The wheel is painful,
and every town I come upon
is a place a man could settle.
It is wonderful
to be as nameless as a mountain
on the other side of the moon,
to be so unprovably myself
that I could be anyone:
an arsonist, an astronaut,
or even a better man.
My car is full of gas.
I signal the opposite
of where it is I'll turn.

THE MAN WHO WAS SAFE

I have never been
the first to applaud for anything.
The women I meet
seem too beautiful to engage,
like cliffs with posted warnings
on the edge of a roily sea.
I have settled for the safe
and the ignominious:
the opinions of my parents
and my pork well-done.
I do not know the flash
of jewels in a dangerous palm,
nor can I comprehend
the adrenaline of risk
or the satisfaction
of failing to achieve
great and implausible things.
When a storm piles up,
the lightning strikes
wherever I am not looking.

THE MAN WITHOUT PASSION ARRIVES
AT THE GRAND CANYON

Year by year, the women in my office
turned into hags, the best
French wines tasted domestic,
and my world became the dream
of a god grown bored. So here I am,
staring at the Grand Canyon
as if it were a gutter
running down a street I never lived on.
The car next to mine is full
of children senselessly impressed
by the action of water on rock,
and their father turns up Beethoven
till each note is clear
and easily comprehended. I roll up
my window, look across the canyon,
and listen. I came here
to see something amazing, to feel
a seed I no longer know the name of
pop like a tick inside of me.
I don't. And the sun above the canyon
says only that it's hot,
and the river down there,
among the rocks, says it isn't finished,
that I'll have to keep on waiting,
maybe longer than I can.

THE MAN ON THE TOWER

No one in the Arrowhead Pub believed
I had the guts to climb that tower
across the highway. So I tottered to it
at rush hour, waltzing past the men
who sped to their wives
and rented lives. When I gripped them

the rungs were hot
from a sun that kept us
crouched at our beers. I climbed up anyway,
and the cops arrived quicker than I thought
and began to ricochet
like blue marbles from car to car.

I didn't think
a man's desire to ascend
could shock them all into action.
But they were shocked
and pointed their voices toward me,
rerouted the traffic

to clear the road. I'll bet they thought
that I would fall, drowning myself
in someone's windshield.
But they were wrong. I clung to that tower
as if it were a woman
and inched my way toward contact.

The faces in the cars grew indistinct.
The horizon spread with every step
till I could see
where the sun fell down. I didn't stop.
I worked with deaf ears
against gravity and the shouts

of their bullhorn. The tower tapered
and I was pinned against the sky,
pricked with a notion to fly.
I had never been above our town,
had never seemed the focus
of so much pure attention.

Why I clambered down
with the care one takes when stooping
for keys in an unlit room,
I cannot say. But I did.
And the whole pub cheered.
And the traffic began again.

THE MAN WHO INVENTED URINAL MINTS
ATTENDS HIS CLASS REUNION

The business never really took off
until I added colors. I spent
months in my parents' basement
mixing the gelatinous aseptic lumps
until I stunk of something pure.
It was an odor that even now—
almost a decade since I'd handled
the stuff—still lingers on my fingertips
and under my manicured nails.
It got to the point where the secretaries
of the big distributors
became confounded by my presence—
an almost mintiness
creeping in the air
and into their gigantic hairdos—
as I sat in their lobbies
clutching my display urinal
and waiting for the door
to open on a man
who understood public rest rooms.
It didn't take long to convince them,
and with a few modifications—
a hair catcher and the right amount
of drainage—I was set for life.
So here I am, with my rented wife
and a pocketful of fifties,

buying drinks for has-been running backs
and a bitch who wouldn't kiss me.
The men are reminded of my success
whenever they drink too much,
and the women simply whisper
that I'm richer than the ones
they settled for. I play it cocky,
and I'm tempted to tell them all
that their piss is my pennies.
Instead, I stare past them
as they reach for my hand
and make certain to read
their name tags twice.
All night, as the band plays songs
I could have been a lover to
and the women dance younger
than they ever did in school,
I sneak looks down my rented wife's
very low-cut blouse, pat her on the ass
when people are looking, and imagine
their faces on all of my mints,
the sweet disintegration of flushing,
and the checks that arrive
more quickly than they're spent.

THE OTHER MAN

Friends talked of visits I couldn't have made
and seemed to like me better.
The neighborhood dogs I'd always kicked
became perplexed as they gnawed their bones
or came wagging up to my side.
This should have given me some kind of clue
that the years of study were about to end.
You see, he has spent his life
intercepting my mail and perfecting the curls
of my signature. His hair is dyed,
his surgeon is good, and he's learned
to slouch to my height. It all makes sense:
my smiling wife and the way she talks
and wants to do everything for me. This other man
is so dedicated that, if I were to lose a leg
or a handful of fingers, I think he would
appear within hours, similarly maimed
and happy. I've been seeing more and more of him—
out at the mall or cruising down Broad
in a Dodge like mine—stopping at the yellows
and signaling his turns. Lately,
when our eyes meet, he looks at me
with a strange satisfaction
that says he needs no pointers now. So today,
for the first time, I followed this man
wherever he went, tailgating and swerving

all the way, till I found myself
driving my street and pulling up to my house.
I let myself in and stood in the hall
and heard the mirror of my voice
seducing my wife. And then there was quiet.
And then there was laughter.
And then they were making love.
The sex was good and my wife so grateful
that I put the steak knife back,
got in my Dodge, and drove—plotting
the rebuttal to his sensitive hands,
his way with the neighborhood dogs.

THE SILENT MAN SPEAKS

Your mouth yawns
to tell me what the weather's like
in a poplar grove
I've huddled in
ever since this morning.
Your breath is bad
and your facts are off:
mistaking cirrus
for the clearly stratus,
downpour for drizzle,
and lightning for the light
that makes the world worth watching.
You think you have the words
that can render the curve
of this or that woman's breast,
the exact shade of blue
jagging across my temple,
or the reason
a woman can touch you
and make your blood change pace.
You'll know more
by keeping quiet and studying
the twigs and pebbles
of this poplar grove.
But all of this is lost on you
like a forkful of salt

in a gallon of broth.
You continue to say
I'm silent and I'm not—
only patient as a trap
that waits for the wrong rabbit
beneath the right sky
in a world that only a fool
would choose to define with words,
whose meanings are
as tricky as a koan
or a man who knows
how to hide a knife—
like this one here,
strapped to my thigh.
Or is it here? Or here?

THE KILLER EXPLAINS HOW HE IS
WINNING HIS VICTIM OVER

All week, the dog has brought pieces
of the woman I buried
and left them on my porch.
She was a woman
whose arms were ropes of silk
that promised to tie me tightly,
whose perfumed wake
could start the office dreaming
and make the deadlines pass.
But dating her was never right.
She arrived too soon
in a dress that made me sad—
and always with a reason
to avoid my bed
or put away the wine.
She was the kind of woman
I had to kill
and bury in a grave close to my house
while the dog just sniffed and whimpered.
Now here she is again—
arriving in increments, her small bones
polished and partly assembled,
attempting to embrace me
with what I have so far.
I do not punish the dog.

I do not sleep unsoundly.
I waken to eggs and the daily news
and fill my sink with bleach.
The house is dizzy
with her dazzling reek.

THE MAN IN THE CAR
EXPLAINS HIS OBSESSION

I am the man who sits in his car
watching her window
at dark. It does not matter
that her blinds are drawn
or that the shape
of her body behind them
is indistinct as a dream
six hours after waking.
I am content with it—my engine
ticking toward a coolness,
the lope of a neighbor's retriever
nuzzling the trash
along her street, and the random
shadow of her body,
which darkens the closer she comes
to the blinds. I imagine her
setting the clock or sipping tea,
unhitching her bra to read a book—
all the little things we do
when we're beautiful
and do not know
we're being watched. Every night,
five minutes after twelve,
the last light in her house
clicks out. And though it's never

come back on, I wait
till half past one
to take the cool metal
of my key in hand
and twist the car into motion.

THE MAN WHOSE LUCK IS CHANGING

After almost a month of sickness,
bad checks and women
who said no, the spider plant
cuttings have let down their roots
in a jar of water and light.
It has been like this all day:
the TV takes in channels
that used to be tiny storms,
and the crayfish in the tank
has shed its skin
and grown its claw back whole.
Even the laundry brought enough change
for a pint of bourbon
and cigarettes. So here I am, blowing
the best smoke rings of my life
and paying all my bills,
and there is no part of my body
that doesn't feel reborn.
In another hour, when this bourbon
is gone, a woman will knock
on that wooden door. She'll be
gorgeous and paid for and mine
for at least an hour. I'll take her
by storm on the davenport.
I'll call it a lucky life.

THE EX-NEUROTIC'S LOVE SONG

I was the plot
of a made-for-TV movie
missing the first half hour.
I was that
incomprehensible. Over breakfast
you wondered why
I checked the gas stove
seven times each morning.
You wondered why
the faucets were never turned
tightly enough.
I did not know myself.
But I had an inkling
that something happened
back before memory began—
something to do
with order and the way
it falls apart
and the constant shadows
of closets. Before we married
I was simply a man
who had to hang
his shirts just so. My world
was not yet perfect.

THE DISHWASHER

Elbow-deep in a sinkful of grease
with the steam curling up
around my face,
I start and end each night,
and the nights are so long
I've learned how to love
this stack of filthy halos,
smeared with lobster sauce
and a signature of crumbs.
Each night I take what's wrong
and put it right
so someone can make it
wrong again. And the wash sink
keeps getting darker
as I pull up plates
from the rinse sink
as clean and smooth as a girl's thigh.
I've let my hands
pucker with water
till you wouldn't call them hands.
I've tasted the ruby of wine
at the bottom
of a stranger's glass.
And I've learned how to like
the house bread
that no one seems to eat—
the hard little loaves

that taste like dust
and crumble to shale
when you butter them.
It is like this every night,
and when the kitchen closes
I leave the last load
drying it its rack
and scour the stainless steel
of my giant sinks
till they shine like dimes
in a child's palm. I've held
this job for half my life,
and nothing can save you
like quitting time. But sometimes,
walking home down Route 38,
the greasy heat stays with me,
and I think of the rinse sink
and the wash sink—
the one as clear as quartz,
the other opaque
as an eye gone bad
in the side of an old man's head.
At the bottom of my sinks,
among the coffee cups and plates,
are knives and broken glass—
invisible as sharks
that dream the cold Atlantic.

THE LOCAL HISTORIAN RECALLS
HIS DRIVE THROUGH SOUTH JERSEY
AFTER FALLING IN LOVE

Yesterday, driving east on Route 70,
I came within miles
of where the *Hindenburg* exploded
like applause around a table
at the toasting of a marriage.
It was June and the pines were green
in the brilliant air,
which smelled like a million cellists
rosining themselves into symphony.
All signs pointed me toward Lakehurst
and, for all I knew, a plaque
on a runway pried apart by weeds.
I did not imagine the women
tumbling to the ground
like bits of errant fireworks,
and I did not wish for souvenirs
or a book to tell me anything.
I simply kept driving a sun-shot road
till I came to a stop
by the hedges of her house—for once
too empty of another's disaster,
for once too enthralled
in a year that I was living.

II. AN EXPLOSION OF GREEN SURRENDER

STORY OF THE MAN WITH
UNSOLVABLE PROBLEMS

The woman in his heart is a repeating
decimal without a pattern
that confounds him
page after page. His god speaks
only in French, in an accent so bad
he catches nothing
but prepositions and a few big words
that make the world
seem worse than the man
had already imagined. Even his cat
continues to bite him
when its purring is most profound.
It has always been like this,
and at night, among the pines,
the planets and stars
form a crown above his head.
It is his crown—the crown of problems
assigned to the wrong man,
who lives in a world of solutions
drying up faster than the mouths of men
trapped on a raft at sea.

STORY OF THE MAN WITH
NOTHING TO LOSE

He needs so many things
that anything would suffice,
and the immaculate void
in his pockets has begun
to give him succor. His world
is a rudderless world.
He revels in its objects—
its women and coins—
and its insignificant pleasures,
which evade his touch more swiftly
than a flock of finches
twittering on a snowcrust.
He can say with certainty
it's never been this bad. Even
his god has turned his attention
toward a more workable world.
And now his powers are growing.
He will soon be dangerous
like science or absolution.
He has nothing to lose but loss.

STORY OF THE MAN IN THE WINDOW

It was Saturday afternoon
and he was up in his apartment
with binoculars and bourbon,
watching a woman tan herself
on a towel by the public pool.
She was the kind of woman
you find on billboards—
the slippery calf, the corporate smile,
the bikini that's barely there—
all of it adding up to say
that you really should just keep driving,
that you'll never get past
her agent. The man watched anyway,
because there was no beauty
in his life, except that which he saw
across great distances: the stars
of Orion winking in the wind,
the lights of a refinery
he had driven past one night,
and the occasional woman
at the public pool, whose parts
are placed more artfully
than those of a sphinx
or Roman aqueduct. Yes,
he was dying of it, this lack
of tangible beauty. And even

when his bourbon was gone,
and his binoculars refused to focus,
and his brain kept stalling
like a bad motor, the idea of beauty
kept flickering in,
like an errand he couldn't quite recall
that kept him from running
the ones he did.

STORY OF THE ESCAPE ARTIST

There was a man who could
escape from anything:
a safe, handcuffs,
even a brass bed—the mattress
stuffed with TNT.
They'd give him thirty seconds
to pick ten locks
and put out the fuse,
and he always made it,
his audience shrieking
to get backstage.
But then he faced a more
difficult task: a woman
with brown eyes
who had seen his show
from every angle, who understood
his double joints and hidden tools
and how the milky flesh
of his assistant
distracted with lust or envy.
And the man, even as he asked
to marry the woman,
wanted to escape
to where there was only applause
and a skeleton key

for all the rooms of his life.
He smelled the fuses
burning behind her eyes,
and he couldn't
understand why they took so long.

STORY OF THE MAN WAKING UP

A man wakes up and does not
touch the snooze button.
Inside of him
is an urgency so great
that he does not dress
or brush his teeth.

He walks right past his wife,
his coffee and his briefcase
filled with another man,
till he finds himself outside,
naked among the houses
like someone escaped
from the quarantine room.

His neighbors let
their cars warm up
a little bit longer than usual,
the dog next door
is suddenly barkless,
and children are stopping
at a bus stop not theirs.

The man can feel his suburb
clamoring to a pause
as he squishes the dirt

between his toes and rubs his butt
in the lawn. And though the crossing
guard herds the children away,
still the man is
mad with it: the dew and the dirt
and the lawn, his wife
calling from a porch
that might as well be in France.

But even at this moment
of supreme separation
and happiness, there must be
something in his brain
regretting it all—
as if his nudity were
a love letter sent
in a morning of deep despair
and the world had opened him up
and said it hardly knew the man,
that it must be someone else.

STORY OF THE MAN ON THE TRACKS

He is walking the tracks, content
to arrive where he must arrive,
led by the steadiness of iron.
He loves the reek of the ties,
their consoling repetition,
and the polished rails
pointing to the next junction.
He does not concern himself
with what lies to either side
of the tracks—the tall grass
whipping itself into patterns
or the unfamiliar stench
curling from dark puddles.
He thinks only of the woman
who waits in the house
a few miles back behind him.
She is a beautiful disruption
that rearranges furniture,
hides his cigarettes,
and straightens the bills
he has not paid.
He lights a cigarette anyway,
kicks at the stones
that litter the tracks—
the brilliant cherts and granites—

and wonders at the will
it must have taken
to splinter a hill and bring it here.

STORY OF THE GENIUS OF FAILURE

One day a man feels himself
pursued by all that he loves
but cannot love well,

so he steps into the forest
behind his house
to become a blackjack oak.

He feels the sap
push up through his legs.
His arms stiffen

and rise above his head
like an explosion
of green surrender.

From where he is rooted,
the man can see his wife
in the windows of their home,

making their bed,
tucking in the children,
and, finally, checking the clock.

And though the man's body
thickens with rings
and his ankles fuse and plummet

toward bedrock and better water,
and though he has evaded
the bloodhounds and the men

who will dredge the river
behind their property, the man
knows this is a failure

in a list of many failures.
This time, he has failed so well
he has become

the genius of failure,
growing each year
till the yard is shadowed

by weak and dangerous limbs.

STORY OF THE MAN WHOSE TASTES
WERE TOO REFINED

Once there was a man
whose tastes were so refined
that nothing could please him.
He would detect the flaws
in the finest bourbon
and declare it undrinkable,
and the women he met
were always out of proportion—
too much here, too little there,
the wrong color hair
for a particular handbag.
His tastes eventually reduced him
to a mixture of scowls
and uproarious guffaws.
Of course, he considered
suicide—leaving his life
the way he'd left so many movies,
before the repulsively blonde
protagonist was saved—
but there was also the hint
of cowardice to consider,
the carpets he might ruin,
the inherent inability
to revise a bullet's path.

III. SEVERAL SONG-FILLED
MINUTES

STAYING IN LOVE

There is a woman you love
so you set her house on fire
late one Saturday night

to see her descend the trellis
from her second-story bedroom
in her sexiest chemise.

And because she is rich
and there are no other houses
and because you have cut

the phone lines that connect her
to everything but you,
it is up to you to rescue her cat

and put the fire out.
You do and she is grateful,
and she doesn't think to ask

why you are there in her backyard,
reeking of turpentine
with her garden hose unraveled.

The two of you marry,
and you are confident
she cannot leave you,

for you are a man with a mind
for disaster. You spend your life
tinkering with her brakes

or loosening boards
on the steps that lead away from you,
and you are always there

to punish the man
you hired to grab her purse.
Your love for her is only safe

when the world is rigged for ruin.

CONSIDERING MY MUSE

My muse has rancid breath
and plays
with herself, reclining

in the arms of the chandelier
above my desk.
She is forever

a distraction, a moaning
in the air
that perfumes the room

to mustard.
She is not beautiful.
She is a woman

raw in all her parts,
and there is no moment
she will not ruin

with the foulest execration.
When I hear her
I know what not to write.

THE CORNER OF PAST LOVES

He is turning the corner
that should never be turned
but always is, turning
to embrace something
that disappeared like an iceberg
lopped from its glacier,
cooling the sea
with its shrinking skin
till nothing is left
but the memory of ice.
He ignores all this.
In his head there is nothing
but the cheer of trumpets
and the rain of confetti
splashing his mouth,
as if he were an astronaut—
back from the moon
and its waterless rock—
perched on the seat of a limousine
as it crawls
to a mayor down Main Street.
But the woman he wants
has passed the same corner
without remorse or nostalgia.
Yes, he is turning
the corner, dialing the number
he should have forgotten,

and his gesture is full
of stupidity and passion.
He wants only to touch
what he should have touched
fifteen years ago,
to scoop up a girl
he didn't love far enough
and cover himself with her—
letting her melt all over him
and into his bed,
defining his world with wetness.

THE MAMMOTH

You come upon her frozen—
packed like a mammoth
in polar ice
on a suddenly blue
and clear afternoon
forming inside your mind.
At first there is merely
the partial recollection:
the smell of her skin
or the love-name.
And then the ice picks
and hammers,
the chiseling down toward meat.
You find her body
perfectly preserved
and have to set up guards
to keep your dogs
from ruining her. Sometimes
at night, beneath the stars
that have always spun
their gorgeous mystery
around your life,
you comprehend
just how it was
she came to be lodged
in that ice, this creature
you brought down running.

THE PREDICTION

—after Donald Justice

On the day of my death
there will not be a comet
streaking the twilit
sky of Philadelphia
to drag the people
from their couches and beer.
The sun will not blink shut
for several song-filled minutes.
And the stars
will not rearrange themselves
to spell my name
in gaudy celestial sequins.
If anything extraordinary
happens in the sky,
it will be a drunken pilot
mistakenly dropping
his bale of marijuana
through the roof
of St. Mary's convent.
Or perhaps a twenty-pound goose
smashing through
an office window
to land at the feet
of a fat executive,
like a feather-filled pillow
drenched in murder.
And I have no qualms

with any of this.
For I've already bought
my whiskey and the goose
and cut my way
through the airport fence.

THE BOX

The box beneath my bed
is full of tiny pains.
Each night I lift its lid
and look inside, as if testing
a very old bandage.
The pains are still pristine—
none of them are healed
and all of them are warm
like a face that has just been slapped.
I close it up, knowing
this box is a weapon
I don't know how to aim.
It may take years to master.

GRUDGES

I hold my grudges
like I hold my brass antiques—
things to be burnished

and prominently displayed.
There is pleasure
in the fault remembered,

and there is so much time
to remember
that to forget the slap

or the lack of kisses
would be tantamount to leaving
the perfect steak

on its perfect plate
till it grew inedibly cold
in a puddle of blood

and wilted parsley.
So come into my gallery.
Marvel at the shine

of the charger plates and frames,
the radiant burn
of my three brass beds.

Your refusal would be delicious.

POEM AFTER BOUNCING THE RENT CHECK AND WAKING WITH A HANGOVER, WHILE SEARCHING FOR MY CAR KEYS TWENTY MINUTES BEFORE A VERY IMPORTANT INTERVIEW

A sudden jolt.
And the Ferris wheel rolls free
of its axle—a blackened
screaming circle
tumbling over the pier.
This is the story
of your life: disaster,
one after another,
as relentless as debt,
as sudden as a hiccup.
Even now the wires
inside your walls
are frayed and sparking
like a tiny Fourth of July.
Even now the woman you love
is testing the feel
of her ringless finger.
There is no point in preparation.
There is no point in anything.
If it has to, disaster will enter
through drafty cracks
or simply run faster than you.
So open the door
and give it a drink.
Say that it's kept you
waiting.

ON BEING TOLD AGAIN THAT MY POSITION
COULD BE NO FURTHER FROM THE TRUTH

If you are in need of directions
and find me on some corner
slouched against a building
as if I'd lived there all my life,
you must not ask me anything.
For I am that thing that could be
no further from the truth.
The interview north of where I stand
will make me send you south,
and if the faint alarm of logic
flickers in your eyes, I will check
my watch and say I must be going.
If you are an average person
and your landlord has run out
of weeks to give, you won't ask
anyone else, and then I'll resume
my slouch against the building,
already forgetting the landmarks
I invented for you. Oh,
you must not ask about anything—
not love, not god, not even
if your tie is straight. To me
the world is a very flat place.
It is still the thirteenth century,
and everyone I meet is falling off its edge,
reading the maps I make.

FINDING HER

The phone rings. I answer it.
The voice on the other end says
she is the milk
inside a coconut, the furniture
I've always needed. I'm stunned
and tell her of my thirst,
my solitude, my desire
for a beautiful armchair.
She says she likes my voice
and tells me we should meet
by the bank of a reedy pond.
I have a hunch this is the girl
I've been searching for—
the one with good teeth
and a flair for words.
Later that night, I find her
languishing on the bank
in the stance of a velvet recliner,
trilling out Thomas
with the smile of a dentist's daughter.
I say nothing. I wear my silence
like a falling rock
for this girl composed of gravity
and utterly good intentions.

THE PROPOSAL

I've heard it said
that love wouldn't be love
if it couldn't carry one
to crime. And, Baby,
the crimes I'll commit for you.
I'll blow up amusement parks
and drape your body
with bits of that hilarious metal.
I'll drive my Dodge
at top speed—blindfolded—
and send you a scrapbook
of traffic tickets and headlines.
I'll paint the windows black
on every house in the county,
forcing them all
to open their doors
when they want to see your hair.
Perhaps I'll just kick
a very large man
and spit in his plate of oysters,
returning home
with a mouthful of blood
and a need for your perfect hands.
Ah, Baby, if I broke enough necks,
if I made enough bombs,
if I shot enough important men

and got to be placed
in the chapel of death row,
would you marry me
in the prison yard
when all the weeds are blooming?

DEVOTION

When he asked for her hand
in marriage, she hacked it off
with a kitchen knife and laid it

in his lap. Her giving did not end.
Breasts and eyelids followed
and fistfuls of golden hair,

tibias and toes,
the pink balloon of a lung,
and the flesh that padded her hip.

The man accepted them all,
kissing each of her parts in turn.
And when she was nothing

more than a heap of groans
with one blade
waving in the center,

he packed her into his suitcase
and headed for the church,
and then to Niagara Falls.

This he knew was devotion.

LOVE

In any situation
it fumbles from his hands
like a broken machine—

the belts and gears
adjusted wrong—hopping
and sputtering across the floor.

The woman picks it up,
makes it right
with an oily finger,

and sends it back to the man.
But now the machine of love
refuses to idle.

It stalls and overheats.
The man examines it,
tinkers with a knob,

and sets it into motion,
expecting his version of love
to reach the woman

with the simple precision
of a Tonka truck.
It doesn't. It never does.

But the woman picks it up.

LUGGAGE

A woman arrived with all of her luggage
and told me her trip went badly.
Just how badly I didn't understand
till I found the bloody dagger
wrapped in black felt, in a hidden
compartment of her leather hatbox.
But we'd already talked about love
and how a woman could kill a man
with the right amount of absence.
We even imagined our future—the houses
we'd build, how we'd never need
luggage again—and by then, she was
sleeping off a sirloin steak,
a bottle of wine, and the sound
of the finches cheeping in the eaves
as the two of us made love. I got up
from her luggage and walked to the bedroom,
deliberately missing the creaky boards
that lived like doubts in the hallway floor,
till I found myself staring down at her—
letting my eyes move from her ankle
to the tuft between her thighs
to the dreaming lids that quivered
like moths. She was beautiful, with the moonlight
like milk all over her skin
and her hair still tousled with love.
I wanted to believe that our future

was firm, that her body would always wake
with mine. But the dagger was still
in its hatbox, and I recalled its handle
felt good in the grip of my startled palm.

TO MEN IN PURSUIT OF
UNINTERESTED WOMEN

You could vandalize the moon
or crack a century in half
with a brilliant assassination.

You could stand beneath her window
with bats flying out of your mouth
in time to your twanging guitar.

You could discover medicinal plants
and claim it was her face
that led you to their meadow.

You could even empty your wallet
on each of her fingers
and prune away your love

for cigarettes and booze.
You could do all of this,
and still she will not notice you.

It is an awful truth, but the name
you scrawled across that moon
can only make you wince,

when you're married and old
and drunk on your veranda,
unable to recall anything clearly

but that her face seemed bored
and slightly confused
as she pulled her window shut.